muffins
and quick breads

TRIDENT PRESS INTERNATIONAL

Published by:
TRIDENT PRESS INTERNATIONAL
801 12th Avenue South
Suite 302
Naples, FL 34102 U.S.A.
(c)Trident Press
Tel: (941) 649 7077
Fax: (941) 649 5832
Email: tridentpress@worldnet.att.net
Website: www.trident-international.com

Muffins and quick breads
Packaged by R&R Publications Marketing Pty Ltd
Creative Director: Paul Sims
Production Manager: Paul Sims
Food Photography: Warren Webb,
William Meppem, Andrew Elton,
Quentin Bacon, Gary Smith, Per Ericson,
Paul Grater, Ray Joice, John Stewart,
Ashley Mackevicius, Harm Mol,
Yanto Noerianto, Andy Payne.
Food Stylists: Stephane Souvlis, Janet Lodge,
Di Kirby, Wendy Berecry, Belinda Clayton,
Rosemary DeSantis, Carolyn Feinberg,
Jacqui Hing, Michelle Gorry,
Christine Sheppard, Donna Hay.

Recipe Development: Ellen Argyriou,
Sheryle Eastwood, Kim Freedman,
Lucy Kelly, Donna Hay, Anneka Mitchell,
Penelope Peel, Jody Vassallo,
Belinda Warn, Loukie Werle.
Proof Reader: Samantha Calcott

Includes Index
ISBN 1 582 79114 7
EAN 9 781582 791142

First Edition Printed September 2000
Computer Typeset in Humanist 521
& Times New Roman

Printed by APP Printing, Singapore
Film Scanning by PICA Overseas, Singapore

muffins
and quick breads

Nothing beats the taste of home-baked cakes and biscuits. Yet, today many people think of home-baked goodies as nothing more than a delightful memory. This need not be so. This book will show that not only is baking an easy and affordable way to fill lunch boxes and provide snacks for your family, but it is also fun. Here you will find a host of recipes that are easy to make and will bring those distant memories of freshly baked treats back to life.

Baking has never been simpler or more fun than with this selection of quick and easy cakes and bakes. A bowl, a beater and a few minutes in the kitchen is all it takes to fill the house with the homey warmth and aroma that only a homemade muffin, cake or batch of biscuits can provide. There's a recipe in these pages to please everyone and every occasion. So, discover the pleasure of home baking and watch your friends and family return for more.

Techniques

When adding fresh fruit to batter it is best to follow the following advice: Whole berries and chopped fresh fruit are less likely to sink to the bottom of muffins and other quick breads during baking if you dredge them in flour first. Then shake off the excess flour in a colander before adding them to the batter. Besides helping to suspend the fruit evenly throughout the batter, the flour coating keeps moist pieces of fruit from clumping together.

The basic ingredients in muffins – flour, flavourings, perhaps some leavening, and liquid – are the same ones used in almost a dozen other varieties of quick breads. Creating such amazing diversity from a few common staples is largely a matter of adjusting the proportions of dry and liquid ingredients. Use two parts dry to one part liquid ingredients and you get a thicker batter for baking muffins or loaves. Thicker still, with a ratio of dry to liquid ingredients approaching three to one, are soft doughs for cut biscuits and scones.

Muffins and most quick breads are at their best when eaten soon after baking. Those that contain fruit, nuts, vegetables or moderately high amounts of fat stay moist longer than those that are low in fat. If muffins are left over it is best to place in the freezer in an airtight container, where they will keep for up to twelve months.

To reheat, bake the frozen muffins, wrapped in foil, at 175°C/350°F for 15-20 minutes, or until heated through. You may also store quick breads and biscuits in the same manner.

classic bluebeery muffins

muffins

The perfect muffin has a gently

rounded top and golden crust, moist finely grained crumb, an appealing aroma and a satisfying balance of flavour.

Muffins are mini-cakes for busy home bakers — freeze them for brunch treats, quick snacks and school lunch boxes, or when you need to stop and take a well-earned break.

apple
& bran muffins

Method:

1 Sift together flour, nutmeg and baking powder into a bowl. Add bran cereal and sugar and mix to combine.

2 Make a well in centre of flour mixture. Add apples, eggs, yoghurt and oil and mix until just combined.

3 Spoon mixture into twelve greased ¹/₂ cup/ 125mL/4fl oz muffin tins and bake for 15 minutes or until muffins are cooked when tested with a skewer.

Note: The secret to making great muffins is in the mixing – they should be mixed as little as possible. It doesn't matter if the mixture is lumpy, while overmixing the mixture will result in tough muffins.

Makes 12

ingredients

1 ¹/₂ cups/230g/7¹/₂oz wholemeal
(wholewheat) flour
¹/₂ teaspoon ground nutmeg
1 ¹/₂ teaspoon baking powder
¹/₂ cup/30g/1oz bran cereal, toasted
¹/₃ cup/60g/2oz brown sugar
2 green apples, grated
2 eggs, lightly beaten
¹/₄ cup/45g/1¹/₂oz low-fat
natural yoghurt
1 tablespoon polyunsaturated
vegetable oil

Oven temperature 180°C, 350°F, Gas 4

10

apricot
oat-bran muffins

Method:

1 Sift flour and baking powder together into a bowl. Add oat bran, apricots and sultanas, mix to combine and set aside.

2 Combine egg, milk, golden syrup and butter.

3 Add milk mixture to dry ingredients and mix until just combined. Spoon mixture into six greased 1 cup/250ml/8fl oz-capacity muffin tins and bake for 15-20 minutes or until muffins are cooked when tested with a skewer. Serve hot, warm or cold.

Note: Serve this muffin for breakfast or brunch fresh and warm from the oven, split and buttered and perhaps with a drizzle of honey.

Makes 6

ingredients

2 cups/250g/8oz all purpose flour
2 teaspoons baking powder
1 cup/45g/1 1/2oz oat bran
60g/2oz dried apricots, chopped
60g/2oz sultanas
1 egg, lightly beaten
1 1/2 cups/325ml/12fl oz buttermilk
or milk
1/4 cup/60ml/2fl oz golden syrup
90g/3oz butter, melted

blackberry
spice muffins

Photograph opposite

Method:

1 *Sift together wholemeal flour, flour, baking powder and allspice into a bowl. Return husks to bowl. Add sugar, almonds, blackberries and banana and mix to combine.*

2 *Place buttermilk, oil and egg in a bowl and whisk to combine. Stir milk mixture into dry ingredients and mix until just combined.*

3 *Spoon mixture into twelve nonstick ¹/₂ cup/ 125ml/4fl oz-capacity muffin tins and bake for 15-20 minutes or until muffins are cooked when tested with a skewer. Turn onto a wire rack to cool.*

Note: *If buttermilk is unavailable use equal parts of low-fat natural yoghurt and reduced-fat milk instead. This recipe will then make 12-15 muffins and the cooking time will be 12-15 minutes. Alternatively ramekins or small pudding basins can be used to make large muffins.*

Makes 12

ingredients

¹/₂ cup/75g/2¹/₂oz wholemeal
(wholewheat) flour
¹/₂ cup/60g/2oz all purpose flour
1¹/₂ teaspoon baking powder
¹/₂ teaspoon ground allspice
¹/₄ cup/45g/1¹/₂oz brown sugar
60g/2oz ground almonds
185g/6oz blackberries
1 banana, mashed
1 cup/250ml/8fl oz buttermilk
¹/₃ cup/90ml/3fl oz vegetable oil
1 egg, lightly beaten

Oven temperature 190°C, 375°F, Gas 5

mango
bran muffins

Photograph opposite

ingredients

Method:

1 *Sift together flour, baking powder and cardamom into a bowl. Add bran, sugar and mango and mix to combine.*

2 *Place egg whites, milk and oil in a bowl and whisk to combine. Stir milk mixture into flour mixture and mix well to combine.*

3 *Spoon mixture into twelve nonstick ¹/₃ cup/ 90ml/3fl oz-capacity muffin tins and bake for 15-20 minutes or until muffins are cooked when tested with a skewer. Turn onto a wire rack to cool.*

Note: *When fresh mangoes are unavailable, drained, canned mangoes can be used instead.*

Makes 12

1 cup/125g/4oz all purpose flour
2¹/₂ teaspoons baking powder
1 teaspoon ground cardamom
1 cup/45g/1¹/₂oz oat bran
¹/₃ cup/60g/2 oz brown sugar
1 mango, chopped
2 egg whites
³/₄ cup/185ml/6fl oz reduced-fat milk
¹/₄ cup/60ml/2fl oz vegetable oil

Oven temperature 190°C, 375°F, Gas 5

cornbread
muffins

Method:

1 Place flour, cornmeal flour (polenta), Parmesan cheese, baking powder, cumin and chilli powder in a bowl and mix to combine.

2 Make a well in centre of flour mixture, add milk, eggs and oil and mix until just combined.

3 Spoon mixture into twelve greased ¹/₃ cup/ 90mL/3fl oz muffin tins and bake for 30 minutes or until muffins are cooked when tested with a skewer.

Note: Cornmeal flour (polenta) is cooked yellow maize flour and is very popular in northern Italian and southern American cooking. It adds an interesting texture and flavour to baked products such as these muffins and is available from health-food stores and some supermarkets.

Makes 12

ingredients

1¹/₂ cups/185g/6oz all purpose flour
1 cup/170g/5¹/₂oz cornmeal flour (polenta)
45g/1¹/₂oz grated Parmesan cheese
2¹/₂ teaspoon baking powder
1 teaspoon ground cumin
pinch chilli powder
2 cups/500ml/16fl oz buttermilk or low-fat milk
2 eggs, lightly beaten
1 tablespoon polyunsaturated vegetable oil

Oven temperature 190°C, 375°F, Gas 5

Oven temperature 180°C, 350°F, Gas 4

lemon-poppy
seed muffins

Method:

1 Place eggs, sour cream, milk, oil, honey, poppy seeds and lemon rind in a bowl and mix well to combine.

2 Add flour and baking powder to poppy seed mixture and mix until just combined.

3 Spoon mixture into six greased 1 cup/250ml/8fl oz-capacity muffin tins and bake for 25-30 minutes or until muffins are cooked when tested with a skewer. Turn onto wire racks to cool.

4 To make icing, place cream cheese, lemon juice and icing sugar in a food processor and process until smooth. Top cold muffins with icing.

Note: A simple glacé icing is another suitable topping for muffins. To make, sift 1 cup/155g/5oz icing sugar into a bowl, slowly stir in 3 teaspoons warm water and a few drops almond or vanilla essence to make a glaze of drizzling consistency. To vary the flavour, omit the essence and substitute the water with 3 teaspoons citrus juice or a favourite liqueur.

Makes 6

ingredients

2 eggs, lightly beaten
1 cup/250g/8oz sour cream
¹/₂ cup/125ml/4fl oz milk
¹/₄ cup/60ml/2fl oz oil
¹/₄ cup/90g/3oz honey
3 tablespoons poppy seeds
1 tablespoon grated lemon rind
2¹/₄ cups/280g/9oz all purpose flour, sifted
3 teaspoons baking powder
Lemon cream-cheese icing
60g/2oz cream cheese, softened
1 tablespoon lemon juice
³/₄ cup/125g/4oz icing sugar

Oven temperature 180°C, 350°F, Gas 4

choc-rough
muffins

Method:
1 Place butter and sugar in a bowl and beat until light and fluffy. Gradually beat in eggs.
2 Combine flour, baking flour and cocoa powder. Add flour mixture, chocolate chips, coconut and milk to butter mixture and mix until just combined.
3 Spoon mixture into six greased 1 cup/ 250ml/8fl oz-capacity muffin tins and bake for 35 minutes or until muffins are cooked when tested with a skewer.

Note: Muffin tins without a nonstick finish should be greased (and, if desired, also lined with paper baking cups) before use. Nonstick tins do not need lining but may need greasing; follow the manufacturer's instructions.

Makes 6

ingredients

125g/4oz butter, softened
1/2 cup/125g/4oz sugar
2 eggs, lightly beaten
2 cups/250g/8oz all purpose flour, sifted
2 1/4 teaspoons baking powder, sifted
1/4 cup/30g/1oz cocoa powder, sifted
155g/5oz chocolate chips
45g/1 1/2oz shredded coconut
3/4 cup/185ml/6fl oz buttermilk or milk

classic
blueberry muffins

Photograph also appears on page 9

Method:

1 *Sift flour and baking powder together into a bowl, add sugar and mix to combine.*
2 *Combine eggs, milk and butter. Add egg mixture and blueberries to dry ingredients and mix until just combined.*
3 *Spoon mixture into six greased 1 cup/250mL/ 8fl oz-capacity muffin tins. Sprinkle with coffee sugar crystals and bake for 20-30 minutes or until muffins are cooked when tested with a skewer. Turn onto wire racks to cool.*

Note: *Finely shredded orange peel can be added to this mixture to enhance the flavour of the blueberries.*

Coffee sugar crystals are coarse golden brown sugar grains. If unavailable, raw (muscovado) or demerara sugar can be used instead.

Makes 6

ingredients

2¹/₂ cups/315g/10oz all purpose flour
3 teaspoon baking powder
¹/₃ cup/90g/3oz sugar
2 eggs, lightly beaten
1 cup/250ml/8fl oz buttermilk or milk
60g/2oz butter, melted
125g/4oz blueberries
2 tablespoons coffee sugar crystals

Oven temperature 200°C, 400°F, Gas 6

17

potato
sour-cream muffins

Photograph opposite

ingredients

250g/8oz mashed potato
2 eggs, lightly beaten
1 cup/250ml/8fl oz milk
3/4 cup/185g/6oz sour cream
60g/2oz butter, melted
2 1/2 cups/315g/10oz all purpose flour
2 1/2 teaspoons baking powder
3 tablespoons snipped fresh chives

Oven temperature 180°C, 350°F, Gas 4

Method:
1 Place potato in a bowl. Add eggs, milk, sour cream and butter to the bowl and mix well to combine.
2 Combine sifted flour, baking powder and chives. Add to potato mixture and mix until just combined. Spoon mixture into six greased 1 cup/250ml/8fl oz-capacity muffin tins and bake for 25-30 minutes or until muffins are cooked when tested with a skewer. Serve warm or cold.
Note: A properly cooked muffin should have risen well, be slightly domed in the middle (but not peaked!) and be evenly browned. It should also shrink slightly from the sides of the tin.
Makes 6

cheese
& bacon muffins

Photograph opposite

ingredients

4 rashers bacon, chopped
1 egg, lightly beaten
1 cup/250ml/8fl oz milk
1/4 cup/60ml/2fl oz vegetable oil
2 tablespoons chopped fresh parsley
2 cups/250g/8oz all purpose flour, sifted
2 1/2 teaspoons baking powder, sifted
90g/3oz grated tasty (mature Cheddar) cheese

Oven temperature 180°C, 350°F, Gas 4

Method:
1 Place bacon in a frying pan and cook over a medium heat, stirring, until crisp. Remove bacon from pan and drain on absorbent kitchen paper.
2 Place egg, milk, oil and parsley in a bowl and mix to combine. Combine sifted flour, baking powder and cheese. Add flour mixture and bacon to egg mixture and mix until combined.
3 Spoon mixture into twelve greased 1/2 cup/ 125mL/4 fl oz-capacity muffin tins and bake for 20-25 minutes or until muffins are cooked when tested with a skewer. Serve warm or cold.
Note: An accurate oven is essential for successful baking. It should be well insulated and draught-proof, as a discrepancy of a few degrees can ruin baked goods. Regular checking with an oven thermometer helps avoid baking failures.
Makes 12

mini sardine
muffins

Method:

1 *Combine flour, baking powder, lemon thyme and paprika in a bowl. In a separate dish mix, together the egg, oil and milk. Quickly and lightly combine the dry and liquid ingredients. Fold in the sardines. Spoon mixture into lightly greased muffin pans or patty pans. Bake in an oven at 200°C/400°F for 12-14 minutes or until golden. Serve warm.*

Makes 24

ingredients

1 ¹/₂ cups/185g/6oz all purpose flour
2 teaspoons baking powder
1 tablespoon lemon thyme
pinch paprika
1 egg
¹/₄ cup/60ml/2fl oz canola oil
³/₄ cup/180ml/6fl oz milk
110g/4oz can sardines in
tomato sauce, mashed

Oven temperature 200°C, 400°F, Gas 6

mushroom
muffins

Method:

1 Sift flour and baking powder into a large bowl. Mix in mushrooms, rice, cheese and herbs.

2 Make a well in the centre of the dry ingredients. Add the remaining ingredients. Mix until just combined (see note).

3 Spoon mixture into greased muffin tins until three quarters full. Bake in the oven 200°C / 400°F for 25 minutes. Remove from tin. Cool on a wire rack. Serve hot or cold.

Note: Don't worry if not all the flour is incorporated as this gives muffins their characteristic texture. Sixteen strokes is usually enough when mixing.

Makes about 12

ingredients

2 cups/250g/8oz all purpose flour
1 tablespoon baking powder
60g/2oz fresh mushrooms, chopped
1/2 cup/75g/2 1/2oz cooked brown rice
1/2 cup/60g/2oz shredded tasty (mature cheddar) cheese
1 tablespoon parsley flakes
2 teaspoons chives, chopped
125g/4oz margarine, melted
1 cup/250mL/8oz milk
1 egg, beaten

sweet-potato
muffins

Method:

1 Boil or microwave sweet potato until tender, drain well and mash. Set aside to cool.

2 Sift wholemeal (wholewheat) flour, all purpose flour, baking powder and sugar in a bowl and mix to combine. Make a well in centre of flour mixture. Add yoghurt, eggs, vanilla essence, currants and cinnamon and mix until just combined. Fold sweet potato into flour mixture.

3 Spoon mixture into twelve greased ¹/₂ cup/ 125ml/4fl oz-capacity muffin tins and bake for 35 minutes or until muffins are cooked when tested with a skewer.

Note: Make muffins when you have time and freeze them to have on hand for quick snacks. If you take your lunch to work, simply take a muffin out of the freezer in the morning – by mid-morning or lunch time it will be thawed.

Makes 12

375g/12oz sweet potato,
peeled and chopped
¹/₂ cup/75g/2¹/₂oz wholemeal
(wholewheat) flour
1 cup/125g/ oz all purpose flour
2 teaspoons baking powder
¹/₃ cup/60g/2oz brown sugar
1 cup/200g/6¹/₂oz low-fat
natural yoghurt
2 eggs, lightly beaten
1 teaspoon vanilla essence
3 tablespoons currants
1 teaspoon ground cinnamon

Oven temperature 190°C, 370°F, Gas 5

sticky
date muffins

Method:

1 Sift flour, bicarbonate of soda and cinnamon together into a bowl. Set aside.
2 Place sugar, butter and dates in a saucepan and heat over a low heat, stirring constantly, until butter melts. Pour date mixture into dry ingredients, add egg and milk. Mix until just combined.
3 Spoon mixture into six greased 1 cup/250ml/ 8fl oz-capacity muffin tins and bake for 30 minutes or until muffins are cooked when tested with a skewer.
4 To make sauce, place butter, sugar, golden syrup and brandy in a saucepan and heat over a low heat, stirring constantly, until sugar dissolves. Bring to the boil, then reduce heat and simmer for 3 minutes or until sauce is thick and syrupy. Serve with warm muffins.
Note: If 1 cup/250 ml/8 oz capacity muffin tins are unavailable, use the standard 1/2 cup/125ml/4fl oz-capacity tins and bake for approximately half the recommended time. The yield, of course, will be doubled.
These muffins make a delicious dessert treat, but are just as good in lunch boxes and for snacks without the sauce.

Makes 6

ingredients

2 cups/250g/8oz all purpose flour
2 teaspoon baking powder
1 teaspoon bicarbonate of soda
(baking soda)
1 teaspoon ground cinnamon
1/3 cup/60g/2oz brown sugar
90g/3oz butter
125g/4oz chopped dates
1 egg, lightly beaten
1 cup/250ml/8fl oz buttermilk or milk
<u>**Brandy sauce**</u>
100g/3 1/2oz butter
1/4 cup/45g/1 1/2oz brown sugar
1 tablespoon golden syrup
1 tablespoon brandy

23

banana
choc-chip muffins

Method:

1 In a mixing bowl, mash the banana, add the milk, egg and melted margarine. Mix well. Stir the sifted flour, baking powder, sugar and choc bits into the banana mixture, mix only until the ingredients are combined. Spoon mixture into well-greased muffin tins. Bake in an oven 190°C/370°F for 20 minutes. Serve warm or cold.

Makes 12

ingredients

1 large ripe banana
1 cup/240ml/8fl oz milk
1 egg
1/4 cup/60ml/2fl oz margarine, melted
1 1/2 cups/185g/6oz all purpose flour
1 1/2 teaspoons baking powder
1/2 cup/120g/4oz caster sugar
3/4 cup/120g/4oz choc bits

oat-bran
fruit muffins

Method:

1. Combine sifted flour, baking powder, oat bran and brown sugar. Beat oil and eggs together and stir in the dry ingredients along with the fruit medley and buttermilk. Mix until just combined, do not over mix.

2. Spoon mixture into lightly greased muffin tins. Bake in an oven 190°C/370°F for 25-30 minutes.

   Makes 12

1 1/2 cups/185g/6oz all purpose flour
2 teaspoons baking powder
1/2 cup/60g/2oz oat bran
1/2 cup/75g/2 1/2oz brown sugar
1/2 cup/120ml/4fl oz canola oil
2 eggs
1/2 cup/90g/3oz fruit medley
1 cup buttermilk

Oven temperature 190°C, 370°F, Gas 5

olive soda bread

quick breads

Quick breads, true to their name,

are quick and easy to bake. They use baking powder or bicarbonate of soda (baking soda) instead of yeast as the rising agent. In this chapter, you will find recipes for such delicious quick breads as bacon-cornbread pots, herb rolls, and carrot and sesame muffins.

blue cheese
& walnut damper

Method:

1 Place sifted flour, baking powder, blue cheese, chives, paprika and 125g/4oz walnuts in a bowl and mix to combine.

2 Make a well in the centre of flour mixture, add milk and oil and mix to form a soft dough.

3 Turn dough onto a lightly floured surface and knead until smooth. Roll into a large ball, flatten slightly and place on a lightly greased baking tray. Sprinkle with Parmesan cheese and remaining walnuts and bake for 40 minutes or until damper is cooked.

Note: This loaf tastes wonderful served hot with hearty soups or at room temperature as part of a cheese and fruit board.

Makes 1 damper

2¹/₂ cups/315g/10oz all purpose flour, sifted
2¹/₂ teaspoons baking powder
220 g/7 oz blue cheese, crumbled
1 tablespoon snipped fresh chives
1 teaspoon paprika
155g/5oz walnuts, chopped
1 cup/250ml/8fl oz buttermilk or milk
1 tablespoon walnut or vegetable oil
60g/2oz grated Parmesan cheese

Oven temperature 180°C, 350°F, Gas 4

cheesy
herb bread

Method:

1 Place flour, baking powder, salt, stock powder, rosemary, dill, chives, sage and 12g/4oz cheese in a bowl and mix to combine.

2 Combine egg, milk and butter. Add egg mixture to dry ingredients and mix to combine.

3 Spoon mixture into a greased and lined 11x21cm/4¹/₂inx8¹/₂in loaf tin, sprinkle with remaining cheese and bake for 45 minutes or until cooked when tested with a skewer. Turn onto a wire rack to cool.

Note: Another time, try combining the flavours of thyme, bay leaves and fennel seeds with the rosemary and sage for a loaf infused with the classic 'herbes de Provence'.

Makes one 11x21cm/4¹/₂x8¹/₂in loaf

ingredients

2 cups/250g/8oz all purpose flour, sifted
2 teaspoons baking powder
1 teaspoon salt
1 teaspoon chicken stock powder
2 tablespoons chopped fresh rosemary or
1 teaspoon dried rosemary
2 tablespoons chopped fresh dill
2 tablespoons snipped fresh chives
2 tablespoons chopped fresh sage or
1 teaspoon dried sage
185g/6oz grated tasty (mature Cheddar) cheese
1 egg, lightly beaten
155ml/5fl oz milk
30g/1oz butter, melted

29

olive
soda bread

Photograph on right and page 27

Method:

1 Place butter, sugar and egg in a food processor and process until smooth. Add wholemeal (wholewheat) flour, flour, bicarbonate of soda, baking powder and milk and process to form a soft dough.

2 Turn dough onto a lightly floured surface and knead in olives. Shape dough into a 20cm/8in-round and place on a lightly greased and floured baking tray. Using a sharp knife, cut a cross in the top. Sprinkle with fennel seeds and salt and bake for 45 minutes or until cooked.

Note: The famous Irish soda bread is influenced here by the Mediterranean flavours of fennel and olives. You may use one of the many types of marinated olives available, if you wish.

Makes one 20cm/8in round loaf

Oven temperature 200°C, 400°F, Gas 5

ingredients

125g/4oz butter, softened
1/4 cup/60g/2oz sugar
1 egg
3 cups/470g/15oz wholemeal (whole wheat) flour
3 teaspoons baking powder
1 1/2 cups/185g/6oz flour
1 1/2 teaspoons bicarbonate of soda (baking soda)
1 1/2 cups/375ml/12fl oz buttermilk or milk
125g/4oz black olives, chopped
2 teaspoons fennel seeds
1 teaspoon coarse sea salt

basil-beer
bread

Photograph opposite

ingredients

Method:

1 Place flour, baking soda, sugar, basil, peppercorns and beer in a bowl and mix to make a soft dough.

2 Place dough in a greased and lined 11x21cm/4 1/2x8 1/2in loaf tin and bake for 50 minutes or until bread is cooked when tested with a skewer.

3 Stand bread in tin for 5 minutes before turning onto a wire rack to cool. Serve warm or cold.

Note: This bread is delicious served spread with olive or sun-dried tomato paste. Any beer may be used here; you can experiment with light and dark ales and even stout to achieve different results.

Makes one 11x21cm/4 1/2x8 1/2in loaf

3 cups/375g/12oz all purpose flour, sifted
3 teaspoons baking powder
1/4 cup/60g/2oz sugar
6 tablespoons chopped fresh basil
1 teaspoon crushed black peppercorns
1 1/2 cups/375ml/12fl oz beer, at room temperature

Oven temperature 160°C, 325°F, Gas 3

shortbread

Method:

1 *Place butter, sugar and vanilla essence in a bowl and beat until light and fluffy. Add flour and rice flour (ground rice) and mix to combine.*
2 *Roll out dough on a lightly floured surface to form a 2cm/³⁄₄in-thick circle.*
3 *Pinch edges or press dough into a large shortbread mould. Place on a lightly greased baking tray and bake for 25 minutes or until lightly browned.*
   Note: *Butter shortbread originated in Scotland as a festive confection particularly for Christmas and Hogmanay.*
   Makes 1 large shortbread round

ingredients

200g/6¹⁄₂oz butter, softened
¹⁄₂ cup/100g/3¹⁄₂oz caster sugar
1 teaspoon vanilla essence
2¹⁄₄ cups/280g/9oz flour, sifted
**¹⁄₃ cup/60g/2oz rice flour
(ground rice), sifted**

Oven temperature 160°C, 325°F, Gas 3

Oven temperature 220°C, 425°F, Gas 7

cornbread

Method:

1 Sift flour with baking powder and salt. Stir in sugar and cornmeal. Add eggs, milk and melted butter. Beat until just smooth.

2 Pour into a 23x23x5cm/9"x9"x2"in tin lined with baking paper and bake in 220°C/440°F oven for 20-25 minutes.

3 Remove from tin and cut into squares to serve with butter.

Serves 4

ingredients

125g/4oz sifted plain flour
4 teaspoons baking powder
³/₄ teaspoon salt
30g/1oz sugar
125g/4oz yellow cornmeal
2 eggs
1 cup/250mL/8oz milk
30g/1oz butter
butter, to serve

easy
berry bread

1

2   3

ingredients

Easy berry bread
3 cups/375g/12oz all purpose flour
1 1/2 teaspoons ground mixed spice
4 teaspoon baking powder
1 1/2 tablespoons sugar
30g/1oz butter
1/2 cup/170ml/5 1/2 fl oz water
1/2 cup/125ml/4fl oz milk
200g/6 1/2oz raspberries
1 tablespoon caster sugar
4 teaspoons milk

Method:

1 Sift flour, mixed spice and baking powder together into a bowl. Add sugar then, using your fingertips, rub in butter until mixture resembles coarse breadcrumbs.

2 Make a well in the centre of flour mixture then, using a round-ended knife, mix in water and milk and mix to form a soft dough.

3 Turn dough onto a floured surface and knead lightly until smooth. Divide dough into two portions and flatten each into an 18cm/ 7in round.

4 Sprinkle raspberries and sugar over surface of one round leaving 2.5cm/1in around edge. Brush edge with a little milk and place remaining round on top. Seal edges securely using fingertips.

5 Place on a greased and lightly floured baking tray. Brush surface of loaf with a little milk a nd bake for 10 minutes. Reduce oven temper ature to 180°C/350°F/Gas 4 and bake for 20-25 minutes longer or until cooked.

Note: Butter absorbs other odours easily, so when keeping it in the refrigerator ensure that it is covered and away from foods such as onions and fish or you will have a strong-smelling butter that will affect the taste of baked goods.

Makes one 18cm/7in round

cheese
& bacon damper

Method:

1 *Rub the margarine into the flour and baking powder until mixture resembles coarse breadcrumbs.*
2 *Stir in parsley, chives, cheese and bacon, mix well.*
3 *Combine the egg and milk, stir into the dry ingredients and mix to a soft dough.*
4 *Turn dough onto a lightly floured board and knead lightly.*
5 *Shape into a cob, cut a deep cross in the centre of the cob and place on a sheet of baking paper on an oven tray.*
6 *Bake in the oven at 200°C/400°F for 30 minutes or until hollow-sounding when tapped underneath.*
7 *Serve hot with a crock of butter on a buffet table, cut into small pieces.*

Serves 6-8

ingredients

3 tablespoons margarine or butter
2¹/₂ cups all purpose flour
3 teaspoons baking powder
2 teaspoons parsley flakes
I teaspoon chopped chives
I cup/125g/4oz grated tasty (mature Cheddar) cheese
2 rashers cooked bacon, finely chopped
I egg
³/₄ cup/180ml/6fl oz milk

Oven temperature 200°C, 400°F, Gas 6

potato
scones

Method:
1 Sift the flour, baking powder and salt together, then rub in the margarine. Beat the eggs and milk together and add to flour mixture to make a firm dough.
2 Add finely mashed potatoes, spring onions and pepper. Stir through lightly. Turn onto a floured board or sheet of non-stick oven paper, knead, then roll out to 1cm/½ in thickness. Cut into rounds and bake in 230°C/450°F oven for 30 minutes. Split open while hot and spread with butter and serve.

Serves 6-8

ingredients

1½ cups/185g/6oz plain flour
1 teaspoon baking powder
½ teaspoon salt
½ cup/125g/4oz margarine
2 eggs, beaten
3/8 cup/100ml/3oz milk
125g/4oz cold mashed potato
3 spring onions, finely chopped
ground black pepper
flour, for kneading
butter, for spreading

Oven temperature 230°C, 450°F, Gas 8

cheese
& onion scones

Method:

1 *Sift flour, baking powder, salt and cayenne. Rub margarine or butter into flour. Add grated cheese, parsley and onion and mix well.*

2 *Make a well in the centre and add beaten egg and milk all at once, and mix quickly to a soft dough. Turn out on a floured board and knead just enough to make a smooth surface.*

3 *Roll to 1cm/¹/₂in thickness and cut into rounds. Place on a floured tray, glaze tops with milk or beaten egg and milk. Bake in a hot oven 230°C/450°F for 10-15 minutes or until scones are browned.*

Serves 6

ingredients

500g/1 lb all purpose flour
4 teaspoons baking powder
1 teaspoon salt
¹/₄ teaspoon cayenne pepper
60g/2oz margarine or butter
100g/3oz grated cheese
1 tablespoon finely chopped parsley
1 dessertspoon finely chopped onion
1 egg, beaten
1 ¹/₂ cups milk

scones

Method:

1 Sift together flour and baking powder into a large bowl. Stir in sugar, then rub in butter, using fingertips, until mixture resembles coarse breadcrumbs.

2 Whisk together egg and milk. Make a well in centre of flour mixture, pour in egg mixture and mix to form a soft dough. Turn onto a lightly floured surface and knead lightly.

3 Press dough out to a 2cm/³/₄in thickness, using palm of hand. Cut out scones using a floured 5cm/2in cutter. Avoid twisting the cutter, or the scones will rise unevenly.

4 Arrange scones close together on a greased and lightly floured baking tray or in a shallow 20cm/8in-round cake tin. Brush with a little milk and bake for 12-15 minutes or until golden.

ingredients

2 cups/250g/8oz all purpose flour
3 teaspoon baking powder
2 teaspoons sugar
45g/1¹/₂oz butter
1 egg
¹/₂ cup/125ml/4fl oz milk

Note: To grease and flour a cake tin or baking tray, lightly brush with melted butter or margarine, then sprinkle with flour and shake to coat evenly. Invert on work surface and tap gently to remove excess flour.

Makes 12

Oven temperature 220°C, 425°F, Gas 7

mini savoury
croissants

Photograph on right

1

ingredients

250g/8oz prepared puff pastry
I egg, lightly beaten with
I tablespoon water
<u>**Asparagus and cheese filling**</u>
60g/2oz Gruyère cheese, grated
4 stalks fresh asparagus, blanched and
finely chopped
paprika freshly ground
black pepper

2

3

Method:

1 *To make filling, place cheese, asparagus, paprika and black pepper to taste in a bowl and mix to combine.*

2 *Roll out pastry to 0.3cm/¹/₈in thick and cut into 10cm/4in-wide strips. Cut each strip into triangles with 10cm/4in bases.*

3 *Place a little filling across the base of each triangle, roll up from the base and mould into a croissant shape. Brush with egg mixture.*

4 *Place croissants on greased baking trays andbake for 12-15 minutes or until puffed and golden. Serve hot or cold.*

Ham and cheese croissants:

Melt 15g/¹/₂oz butter in a frying pan and cook 100g/3¹/₂oz finely chopped ham and 2 finely chopped spring onions over a medium heat for 3-4 minutes or until onions are soft. Remove from heat, stir in 2 teaspoons finely chopped parsley and black pepper to taste. Cool. Assemble, sprinkling filling with 45g/1¹/₂oz tasty (mature Cheddar) cheese and cook as directed.

Chocolate croissants:

Use 45g/1¹/₂oz grated milk or dark chocolate to fill triangles. Assemble and cook as directed.

Note: *Puff pastry always gives a spectacular result and no more so than in these mini croissants. The secret with these savoury delights is in the shape. Follow the step-by-step instructions to make the quickest and tastiest treats ever.*

Makes 12

41

simple
wholemeal loaf

Method:

1 *Sift flour, then mix in the wholemeal flour. Make a well in the centre, crumble in the yeast, add the sugar and 3 tablespoons of the water. Stand in a warm place for 15 minutes.*

2 *Add the rest of the water and salt and make dough. Knead well on a floured board, place in a well-greased tin and stand in a warm place for 40 minutes to let rise.*

3 *Bake in a hot oven 220°C/440°F with decreasing heat and cook for 1½ hours.*

Serves 4

ingredients

**2cups/250g/8oz all purpose flour, sifted
2cups/250g/8oz wholemeal flour
15g/½ oz compressed yeast
½ teaspoon sugar
1 teaspoon salt
1¼ cups/310ml/10oz tepid water
extra flour, for kneading**

Oven temperature 220°C, 425°F, Gas 7

banana bread

Method:

1 *Cream the butter and sugar. Add the eggs, bananas and flour with salt and soda.*

2 *Place into a greased loaf tin and bake 45 minutes in a 180°C/350°F oven. Serve hot or cold, sliced and spread with butter.*

Serves 4

Oven temperature 180°C, 350°F, Gas 4

ingredients

**125g/4oz butter
½ cup/125g/4oz caster sugar
2 eggs
3 mashed bananas
2cups/250g/8oz plain flour
¼ teaspoon salt
¾ teaspoon bicarbonate of soda
extra butter, for spreading**

coffee rolls

Method:

1 *Beat butter and sugar till creamy, add egg and milk. Sift the flour with the soda and cream of tartar and fold in. Roll out, cut into small squares, then roll each piece over 3 times.*

2 *Brush with the white of an egg or a little milk and bake in a hot oven 220°C/440°F until cooked.*

Serves 4

ingredients

**1 heaped tablespoon butter
1 large tablespoon sugar
1 egg
1 cup/250ml/8oz milk
2cups/250g/8oz plain flour
1 teaspoon bicarbonate of soda
2 teaspoons cream of tartar**

Oven temperature 220°C, 425°F, Gas 7

griddle cakes

Method:

1 Beat egg and sugar till creamy, sift the flour, baking powder and add salt. Stir in the milk until mixture drops easily from a spoon.
2 Heat a heavy frying pan, add a small knob of butter and when melted drop mixture by the spoonful. Turn when cooked on one side.

Serves 2

ingredients

1 egg
2 teaspoons sugar
125g/4oz plain flour
1 teaspoon baking powder
pinch salt
3/4 cup/185ml/6oz milk
30g/1oz butter

rock cakes

Method:

1 Place flour, baking powder and sugar in a bowl. Rub in butter, using fingertips, until mixture resembles fine breadcrumbs. Stir in dried fruit, lemon rind and orange rind. Add egg and milk and mix to form a soft dough.
2 Place tablespoons of mixture on greased baking trays and spinkle lightly with cinnamon-sugar mixture. Bake for 12-15 minutes or until golden. Transfer to wire racks to cool.
Note: Do not sore different types of biscuits together as they will absorb flavours and moisture from each other.

Makes 30

ingredients

2cups/250g/8oz plain flour, sifted
2 1/2 teaspoons baking powder
1/4 cup/60g/2oz caster sugar
90g/3oz butter
125g/4oz mixed dried fruit, chopped
1 teaspoon finely grated lemon rind
1 teaspoon finely grated orange rind
1 egg, lightly beaten
1/3 cup/90ml/3fl oz milk
1/2 teaspoon cinnamon mixed with
2 tablespoons caster sugar

Oven temperature 180°C, 350°F, Gas 4

soda bread

Photograph on page 46

4 cups/500g/1 lb flour
1 teaspoon bicarbonate of soda
1 teaspoon salt
45g/1½oz butter
2 cups/500ml/16fl oz buttermilk
or milk

Method:

1 *Sift together flour, bicarbonate of soda and salt into a bowl. Rub in butter, using fingertips, until mixture resembles coarse breadcrumbs. Make a well in the centre of the flour mixture and pour in milk and, using a round-ended knife, mix to form a soft dough.*

2 *Turn dough onto a floured surface and knead lightly until smooth. Shape into an 18cm/7in round and place on a greased and floured baking tray. Score dough into eighths using a sharp knife. Dust lightly with flour and bake for 35-40 minutes or until loaf sounds hollow when tapped on the base.*

Note: *A loaf for when you need bread unexpectedly, Soda Bread is made with bicarbonate of soda rather than yeast so it requires no rising. It is best eaten slightly warm and is delicious with lashings of treacle or golden syrup.*

Serves 8

Oven temperature 200°C, 400°F, Gas 6

fig scones

2cups/250g/8oz plain flour
2¼ teaspoons baking powder
65g/2oz sugar
¾ teaspoon salt
125g/4oz butter
65g/2oz finely chopped dried figs
2 eggs, slightly beaten
milk, for brushing
cinnamon and sugar, for glaze

Method:

1 *Sift all dry ingredients together. Rub in the butter, add the figs and the slightly beaten egg. Stir with a fork until mixture forms a soft ball.*

2 *Roll out onto a lightly floured board about 1cm/½in thick and cut into triangles or rounds. Brush tops with a little milk, sprinkle with sugar and cinnamon and bake in a hot oven 200°C/400°F until golden brown, about 15 minutes.*

Serves 3-4

Oven temperature 200°C, 400°F, Gas 6

chilli-soup biscuits

Method:

1 Cook bacon in a nonstick frying pan over a medium-high heat for 3-4 minutes or until crisp. Remove from pan and drain on absorbent kitchen paper.

2 Sift together flour, baking powder and salt into a bowl. Rub in butter with fingertips until mixture resembles coarse breadcrumbs.

3 Stir bacon, cheese and chillies into flour mixture. Add milk and mix to form a soft dough. Turn onto a lightly floured surface and knead lightly with fingertips until smooth.

4 Using heel of hand, gently press dough out to 1cm/¹/₂in thickness. Cut out rounds using a 5cm/2in pastry cutter. Place on a greased baking tray and brush with melted butter. Bake for 12-15 minutes or until golden brown. Remove from tray and cool on a wire rack or serve warm spread with butter.

Makes 16

ingredients

2 rashers bacon, finely chopped
2 cups/250g/8oz flour
3 teaspoons baking powder
¹/₂ teaspoon salt
90g/3oz butter
90g/3oz grated tasty
(mature Cheddar) cheese
2 small fresh red chillies, seeded and
finely chopped
²/₃ cup/170mL/5¹/₂fl oz milk
30g/1oz butter, melted

Oven temperature 220°C, 425°F, Gas 7

herb rolls

Method:

1 Melt butter in a frying pan and cook spring onions over a medium heat for 2-3 minutes or until soft. Remove from heat and set aside.

2 Sift together flour and self-raising flour, baking powder and bicarbonate of soda into a large bowl. Stir in sugar, parsley and basil. Combine milk, eggs and onion mixture and mix into flour mixture to form a firm dough.

3 Turn onto a floured surface and knead lightly until smooth. Divide dough into twelve equal portions, then roll each portion into a ball and place on greased and floured baking trays. Brush each roll with egg and oil mixture and bake for 30-35 minutes or until golden and cooked through.

Note: Spring onions and herbs have been added to this soda bread recipe. The dough is then formed into rolls to make the quickest herb-flavoured rolls ever.

Makes 12

ingredients

90g/3oz butter
8 spring onions, finely chopped
2¹/₂ cups/315g/10oz flour
1 cup/125g/4oz self-raising flour
3 teaspoons baking powder
¹/₂ teaspoon bicarbonate of soda
4 teaspoons sugar
1 tablespoon finely chopped
fresh parsley
1 tablespoon finely chopped fresh basil
¹/₂ cup/125mL/4fl oz buttermilk or milk
3 eggs, lightly beaten
1 egg, beaten with 1¹/₂ tablespoons
olive oil

Oven temperature 180°C, 350°F, Gas 4

herb
& cheese loaf

ingredients

Method:

1 *Place flour, baking powder, rolled oats, bran, tasty (mature Cheddar) cheese, Parmesan cheese, chives and parsley in a bowl and mix to combine. Make a well in the centre of the flour mixture, add milk and oil and mix well to combine.*

2 *Place egg whites in a clean bowl and beat until stiff peaks form. Fold egg whites into batter.*

3 *Spoon batter into a greased and lined 11x21cm/ 4¹/₂x8¹/₂in loaf tin and bake for 40 minutes or until cooked when tested with a skewer.*
Note: *This high-fibre loaf is terrific served warm.*
Makes one 11x21cm/4¹/₂x8¹/₂in loaf

ingredients

1¹/₄ cups/185g/6oz wholemeal (wholewheat) flour
1¹/₄ teaspoon baking powder
1 cup/90g/3oz rolled oats
45g/1¹/₂oz unprocessed bran
60g/2oz grated tasty (mature Cheddar) cheese
1 tablespoon grated Parmesan cheese
2 tablespoons snipped fresh chives
2 tablespoons chopped fresh parsley
1 cup/250ml/8fl oz milk
¹/₃ cup/90ml/3fl oz vegetable oil
3 egg whites

Oven temperature 180°C, 350°F, Gas 4

carrot
& sesame muffins

Method:

1 *Sift together flour, baking powder, bicarbonate of soda and mixed spice into a large bowl. Add sugar, carrot, sesame seeds and sultanas and mix to combine.*

2 *Place yoghurt, milk, butter and egg whites in a bowl and whisk to combine. Stir yoghurt mixture into flour mixture and mix until just combined. Spoon batter into lightly greased muffin tins and bake for 20 minutes or until golden and cooked.*
Note: *Delicious light muffins are perfect weekend fare. Any leftovers can be frozen and used when time is short.*
Makes 24

ingredients

3 cups/375g/12oz all purpose flour
3¹/₂ teaspoons baking powder
¹/₂ teaspoon bicarbonate of soda (baking soda)
1 teaspoon ground mixed spice
¹/₂ cup/90g/3oz brown sugar
1 large carrot, grated
4 tablespoons toasted sesame seeds
170g/5¹/₂oz sultanas
1 cup/200g/6¹/₂oz natural yoghurt
1 cup/250ml/8fl oz milk
3 tablespoons melted butter
3 egg whites, lightly beaten

Oven temperature 200°C, 400°F, Gas 6

bacon
cornbread pots

Method:

1 Cook bacon in a nonstick frying pan over a medium heat for 3-4 minutes or until crisp. Remove bacon from pan and drain on absorbent kitchen paper.

2 Place cornmeal flour (polenta), flour, baking powder, sugar, salt, Parmesan cheese and butter in a food processor and process until mixture resembles fine breadcrumbs.

3 Combine eggs and milk and, with machine running, pour into cornmeal (polenta) mixture and process until combined and batter is smooth. Take care not to overmix. Stir in bacon.

4 Spoon batter into three medium-sized terracotta flowerpots lined with well-greased aluminium foil. Place on a baking tray and bake for 25-30 minutes or until golden.

Note: Cooked in flowerpots these tasty cornbread loaves are a perfect accompaniment to soup or salad. Remember that the size of the flowerpots you use will determine the number of loaves you produce.

Serves 6
Makes 3 medium-sized flowerpot loaves

Oven temperature 200°C, 400°F, Gas 6

ingredients

4 rashers bacon, finely chopped
1 1/2 cups/250g/8oz fine cornmeal flour (polenta)
1 cup/125g/4oz flour
2 1/2 teaspoons baking powder
4 teaspoons sugar
1/2 teaspoon salt
60g/2oz grated Parmesan cheese
90g/3oz butter, chopped
2 eggs, lightly beaten
1 1/4 cups/315ml/10fl oz buttermilk or milk

monte carlo

cookies and biscuits

In this chapter you will find a wonderful

array of cookies and biscuits and other baked treats. It is easy to understand why this type of baked product is popular. Not only are they easy to make, but they come in a huge variety of flavours and textures. Best of all, they are just the right size for a snack.

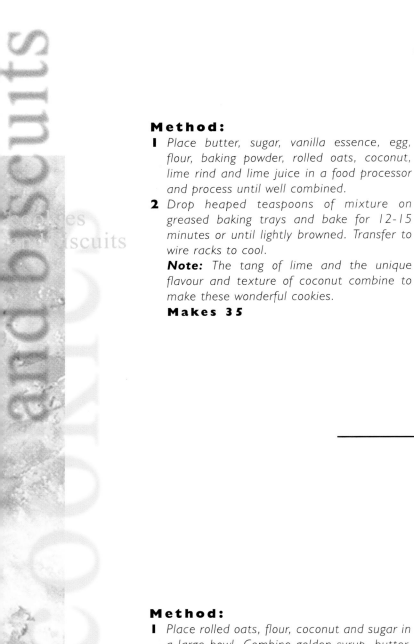

coconut
cookies

Photograph opposite

ingredients

125g/4oz butter, chopped
I cup/170g/5¹/₂oz brown sugar
I teaspoon vanilla essence
I egg
I¹/₂ cup/125g/4oz flour
¹/₂ teaspoon baking powder
I cup/90g/3oz rolled oats
45g/1¹/₂oz desiccated coconut
2 teaspoons finely grated lime rind
2 tablespoons lime juice

Method:

I Place butter, sugar, vanilla essence, egg, flour, baking powder, rolled oats, coconut, lime rind and lime juice in a food processor and process until well combined.

2 Drop heaped teaspoons of mixture on greased baking trays and bake for 12-15 minutes or until lightly browned. Transfer to wire racks to cool.

Note: The tang of lime and the unique flavour and texture of coconut combine to make these wonderful cookies.

Makes 35

Oven temperature 180°C, 350°F, Gas 4

golden
oat biscuits

Photograph opposite

ingredients

I cup/90g/3oz rolled oats
I cup/125g/4oz flour, sifted
90g/3oz desiccated coconut
I cup/250g/8oz sugar
4 teaspoons golden syrup, warmed
125g/4oz butter, melted
2 tablespoons boiling water
I teaspoon bicarbonate of soda

Method:

I Place rolled oats, flour, coconut and sugar in a large bowl. Combine golden syrup, butter, water and bicarbonate of soda.

2 Pour golden-syrup mixture into dry ingredients and mix well to combine. Drop teaspoons of mixture 3cm/1¹/₄in apart on greased baking trays and bake for 10-15 minutes or until biscuits are just firm. Stand on trays for 3 minutes before transferring to wire racks to cool.

Note: Biscuits should always be stored in an airtight container. Allow the biscuits to cool completely on wire cooling racks before storing.

Makes 30

Oven temperature 180°C, 350°F, Gas 4

croissants

Method:

1 Sift flour onto a board and divide into four. Take one quarter and make a well in the centre. Place the yeast in this and mix with about 2-3 tablespoons warm milk-and-water mixture. The yeast must be dissolved and the dough soft.

2 Have ready a saucepan of warm water and drop the ball of yeast dough into this and set aside. Add the salt to the rest of the flour, make a well in the centre, add half the butter and work up, adding enough of the milk-and-water mixture to make a firm paste.

3 Beat on the board for about 5 minutes. Lift the yeast dough from the water – it should be spongy and well risen – mix into the paste thoroughly.

4 Turn into a floured bowl, cover with a plate and place in the refrigerator for 12 hours. Roll out the paste to a square, place the rest of the butter in the centre and fold up like a parcel.

5 Give the paste three turns as for puff pastry, and a fourth if the butter is not completely absorbed. Rest the paste between every two turns and chill before shaping.

6 When ready for shaping, roll out very thinly to an oblong shape, divide into two lengthwise and cut each strip into triangles.

7 Roll up each one starting from the base and seal tip with beaten egg. Curl to form a crescent then set on a dampened baking tray. Let stand for about 10 minutes then brush with beaten egg. Bake in a hot oven 200°C/400°F for about 25 minutes.

Serves 4

ingredients

375g/12oz flour
15g/¹/₂oz yeast
¹/₂ teaspoon salt
150mL/5oz warm milk and water (half and half)
185g/6oz butter

Oven temperature 200°C, 400°F, Gas 6

coffee
kisses

250g/8oz butter, softened
¹/₂ cup/100g/3¹/₂oz icing (powdered)
sugar, sifted
2 teaspoons instant coffee powder
dissolved in 1 tablespoon hot
water, cooled
2 cups/250g/8oz flour, sifted
45g/1¹/₂oz dark chocolate, melted
icing (powdered) sugar

Method:

1 Place butter and icing (powdered) sugar in a bowl and beat until light and fluffy. Stir in coffee mixture and flour.

2 Spoon mixture into a piping bag fitted with a medium star nozzle and pipe 2cm/³/₄in rounds of mixture 2cm/³/₄in apart on greased baking trays. Bake for 10-12 minutes or until lightly browned. Stand on trays for 5 minutes before removing to wire racks to cool completely.

3 Join biscuits with a little melted chocolate, then dust with icing sugar.

Note: These coffee-flavoured biscuits have a similar texture to shortbread – making the dough perfect for piping. For something different you can pipe 5cm/2in lengths instead of rounds. Rather than sandwiching the biscuits together with chocolate you might prefer to leave them plain and simply dusted with icing (powdered) sugar.

Makes 25

afghan
biscuits

Method:

1 Place butter and vanilla essence in a bowl and beat until light and fluffy. Gradually add sugar, beating well after each addition until mixture is creamy.

2 Sift together flour, baking powder and cocoa powder. Stir flour mixture into butter mixture, then fold in cornflakes and sultanas. Drop heaped teaspoons of mixture onto greased baking trays and bake for 12-15 minutes. Remove to wire racks to cool completely.

3 To make icing, place butter, cocoa powder and icing (powdered) sugar in a bowl and mix with enough water to make an icing of spreading consistency.

4 Place a little icing on each biscuit and sprinkle with almonds. Set aside until icing firms.

Note: Do not store different types of biscuits together as they absorb flavour and moisture from each other.

Makes 30

200g/6¹/₂oz butter, softened
1 teaspoon vanilla essence
¹/₂ cup/100g/3¹/₂oz caster sugar
1¹/₂ cups/185g/6oz flour
1 teaspoon baking powder
1 tablespoon cocoa powder
90g/3oz cornflakes, crushed
2 tablespoons chopped sultanas
slivered almonds
<u>Chocolate icing</u>
15g/¹/₂oz butter, softened
1 tablespoon cocoa powder
1 cup/155g/5oz icing (powdered) sugar, sifted
1 tablespoon boiling water

Oven temperature 200°C, 400°F, Gas 6

melting
moments

Method:

1 Place butter and icing (powdered) sugar in a bowl and beat until light and fluffy. Sift together cornflour and flour and stir into butter mixture.

2 Spoon mixture into a piping bag fitted with a large star nozzle and pipe small rosettes on greased baking trays, leaving space between each rosette. Bake for 15-20 minutes or until just golden. Allow biscuits to cool on trays.

3 To make filling, place butter in a bowl and beat until light and fluffy. Gradually add icing sugar and beat until creamy. Stir in lemon rind and lemon juice. Sandwich biscuits together with filling.

Note: Grease baking trays with a little vegetable oil. Biscuits should be of a uniform size; not only will they look more attractive but they will also cook more evenly.

Makes 24

250g/8oz butter, softened
4 tablespoons icing sugar, sifted
1 cup/125g/4oz cornflour (cornstarch)
1 cup/125g/4oz flour
<u>Lemon-cream filling</u>
60g/2oz butter, softened
¹/₂ cup/75g/2¹/₂oz icing (powdered) sugar
2 teaspoons finely grated lemon rind
1 tablespoon lemon juice

Oven temperature 180°C, 350°F, Gas 4

ginger
snaps

Method:
1 *Sift brown sugar, ginger and flour together into a bowl.*
2 *Place butter and golden syrup in a saucepan and cook over a low heat, stirring, until butter melts. Stir in bicarbonate of soda. Pour golden-syrup mixture into dry ingredients and mix until smooth.*
3 *Drop teaspoons of mixture onto greased baking trays and bake for 10-12 minutes or until golden. Remove from oven, loosen biscuits with a spatula and allow to cool on trays.*
Note: *As these biscuits cool, they become crisp.*

Makes 45

1 cup/170g/5¹/₂oz brown sugar
3 teaspoons ground ginger
2 cups/250g/8oz flour
125g/4oz butter
1 cup/350g/11oz golden syrup
1 teaspoon bicarbonate of soda

Oven temperature 180°C, 350°F, Gas 4

christmas
cookies

Method:

1 Place butter and sugar in a bowl and beat until light and fluffy. Beat in egg, vanilla essence and milk and continue to beat until well combined.

2 Stir together flour and bicarbonate of soda and stir into butter mixture. Add hazelnuts, chocolate chips, coconut, sultanas and cherries and mix until well combined.

3 Drop tablespoons of mixture onto greased baking trays and bake for 15 minutes or until golden. Remove to wire racks to cool completely.

Note: Glacé fruits such as glacé cherries or pineapple should be rinsed and dried before using in cakes to remove the sugary coating. This will help to prevent the fruit from sinking to the bottom of the cake.

Makes 25

ingredients

125g/4oz butter
1 cup/220g/7oz caster sugar
1 egg, lightly beaten
2 teaspoons vanilla essence
1/4 cup/60mL/2fl oz milk
1 1/4 cups/155g/5oz flour
1/2 teaspoon bicarbonate of soda
90g/3oz roasted hazelnuts, chopped
125g/4oz chocolate chips
90g/3oz shredded coconut
90g/3oz sultanas
90g/3oz glacé cherries, chopped

Oven temperature 180°C, 350°F, Gas 4

cinnamon
crisps

Method:

1 Place butter and ³/₄ cup/170g/5¹/₂oz sugar in a bowl and beat until light and fluffy. Add egg and beat well.

2 Sift together flour, baking powder and bicarbonate of soda and stir into butter mixture. Turn dough onto a floured surface and knead briefly. Wrap in plastic food wrap and refrigerate for 30 minutes or until firm.

3 Place cinnamon and remaining sugar in a small bowl and mix to combine. Roll dough into small balls, then roll balls in sugar mixture. Place 5cm/2in apart on lightly greased baking trays and bake for 8 minutes or until golden. Remove to wire racks to cool.

Note: Fat or shortening in whatever form makes a baked product tender and helps to improve its keeping quality. In most baked goods, top-quality margarine and butter are interchangeable.

Makes 25

ingredients

125g/4oz butter
1 cup/220g/7oz caster sugar
1 egg
1¹/₂ cups/185g/6oz flour
¹/₂ teaspoon baking powder
¹/₂ teaspoon bicarbonate of soda
2 teaspoons ground cinnamon

cashew-nut
cookies

Photograph opposite

Method:

1 *Place butter and sugar in a bowl and beat until light and fluffy. Add vanilla essence and egg yolk and beat to combine.*

2 *Fold flour, baking powder and wheat germ into butter mixture. Turn dough onto a lightly floured surface and knead briefly. Shape into a log, wrap in plastic food wrap and refrigerate for 30 minutes or until firm.*

3 *Slice dough into 0.5cm/1/4in slices and place on greased baking trays. Press a cashew nut into the top of each biscuit and bake for 10-12 minutes or until golden.*

Note: *Toasting nuts increases their flavour. To toast, place on a baking tray and cook at 180°C/350°F/Gas 4 for 5-10 minutes, shaking the tray from time to time. Take care that the nuts do not burn by removing them from the oven as soon as they are golden.*

Makes 48

ingredients

125g/4oz butter
1/3 cup/75g/21/ oz caster sugar
1 teaspoon vanilla essence
1 egg yolk
1 1/2 cups/185g/6oz flour, sifted
3/4 teaspoon baking powder
2 tablespoons wheat germ
60g/2oz unsalted cashew nuts, toasted

Oven temperature 180°C, 350°F, Gas 4

chocolate-
almond balls

Photograph opposite

ingredients

1/2 cup/125ml/4fl oz thickened (double) cream
125g/4oz dark chocolate, chopped
15g1/2oz butter
60g/2oz almonds, finely chopped, toasted
30g/1oz puffed rice cereal, crushed

Method:

1 *Place cream and chocolate in a saucepan and cook over a low heat, stirring, until chocolate melts. Remove pan from heat and set aside to cool slightly. Stir in butter, cover and chill.*

2 *Using an electric mixer, beat chocolate mixture until soft peaks form. Return to the refrigerator until firm.*

3 *Place almonds and rice cereal in a bowl and mix to combine. Shape teaspoons of chocolate mixture into balls and roll in almond mixture. Store in an airtight container in the refrigerator.*

Note: *Served with coffee this uncooked biscuit makes a delicious after-dinner treat.*

Makes 24

Oven temperature 180°C, 350°F, Gas 4

triple choc-chip
cookies

Method:

1 *Cream together sugars, margarine and vanilla essence. Add the egg and beat in well.*
2 *Sift the flour and baking powder together and add to the creamed mixture. Stir in the choc bits, milk bits and white bits.*
3 *Place teaspoonfuls of mixture onto lightly greased oven trays.*
4 *Bake in a 180°C/350°F oven for 15 minutes. Cool on tray 5 minutes before removing to wire tray to cool. Store in airtight container.*

Makes 36

ingredients

$^1/_2$ **cup/120g/4oz caster sugar**
$^1/_2$ **cup/75g/2$^1/_2$oz brown sugar**
175g/6oz margarine
$^1/_2$ **teaspoon vanilla essence**
1 egg
1$^3/_4$ cup/210g/7oz plain flour
1$^1/_2$ teaspoon baking powder
$^1/_2$ **cup/75g/2$^1/_2$oz each choc bits, milk bits and white bits**

Oven temperature 180°C, 350°F, Gas 4

62

peanut
cookies

ingredients

Method:

1 *Cream peanut butter, butter and sugar together until light and fluffy. Add egg and vanilla and mix well. Stir flour and baking powder together and stir into the butter mixture. Mix to a stiff dough and, if necessary, add a little extra flour.*

2 *Take one rounded teaspoon of mixture and roll into a small ball. Repeat with remainder.*

3 *Cover the turntable with a sheet of non-stick baking paper cut to size. Place 10 balls around turntable 2cm/³/₄in in from the edge.*

4 *Flatten slightly with the back of a fork. Cook on high for 2 minutes. Re-press fork marks left on biscuits as soon as they are cooked if desired. Slide paper with biscuits onto a cake cooler and allow to cool before removing from paper. Cook remaining biscuits in the same manner.*

Makes 25-30 biscuits

¹/₂ **cup120g/4oz peanut butter**
90g/3oz butter
³/₄ **cup/180g/6oz sugar**
1 egg
¹/₂ **teaspoon vanilla essence**
1 ¹/₂ **cups/180g/6oz flour**
¹/₂ **teaspoon baking powder**

Oven temperature 180°C, 350°F, Gas 4

pecan
anzacs

Method:

1 *Melt margarine and golden syrup in a saucepan, and add the bicarbonate of soda dissolved in the boiling water.*

2 *Combine the oats, coconut, flour, sugar, and pecans. Pour the melted mixture over the dry ingredients and mix well. Place teaspoonfuls of the mixture onto greased oven trays allowing room for spreading.*

3 *Bake in an oven 160°C/330°C for 15 minutes or until golden. Cool biscuits a few minutes on tray before removing to a wire rack to cool completely.*

4 *Store in an airtight container.*

Makes approximately 48 biscuits

125g/4oz margarine
1 tablespoon golden syrup
1 teaspoon of bicarbonate of soda
2 tablespoons boiling water
1 cup/90g/3oz rolled oats
³/4 cup/65g/2oz desiccated coconut
1 cup/120g/4oz plain flour
1 cup/250g/8oz sugar
¹/3 cup/75g/2¹/2oz chopped pecans

prune & orange
cookies

Method:

1 *Cream together margarine, icing sugar and orange rind, blend in the flour. Stir the prunes through the mixture.*
2 *Roll mixture into small balls and place on a lightly greased oven tray. Flatten with a fork.*
3 *Bake in an oven 180°C/350°F for 12-15 minutes.*
4 *Cool on a tray 5 minutes before removing to a wire rack to cool completely.*
5 *Decorate cookies with melted chocolate.*

Makes 24

ingredients

125g/4oz margarine
1/2 cup/75g/2 1/3oz icing sugar
grated rind of 1 orange
1 cup/120g/4oz plain flour
1/2 cup/120g/4oz prunes, chopped
dark chocolate, melted

Oven temperature 180°C, 350°F, Gas 4

orange-
pistachio biscotti

Method:

1 *Sift together flour, sugar, baking powder and salt into a bowl.*
2 *Place eggs, egg whites, orange rind and vanilla essence in a separate bowl and whisk to combine.*
3 *Stir egg mixture and pistachio nuts into flour mixture and mix to make a smooth dough. Turn dough onto a lightly floured surface and divide into two equal portions. Roll each portion into a log with a diameter of 5cm/2in. Flatten logs slightly and place 10cm/4in apart on a nonstick baking tray. Bake for 30 minutes. Remove from oven and set aside to cool.*
4 *Reduce oven temperature to 150°C/ 300°F/Gas 2.*
5 *Cut cooled logs into 1cm/¹/₂in thick slices, place on nonstick baking trays and bake for 10 minutes or until biscuits are crisp.*

Makes 48

ingredients

2 cups/250g/8oz flour
1 cup/250g/8oz sugar
1 teaspoon baking powder
pinch salt
2 eggs
2 egg whites
1 tablespoon finely grated orange rind
¹/₂ teaspoon vanilla essence
75g/2¹/₂oz pistachios,
shelled and toasted

Oven temperature 180°C, 350°F, Gas 4

Oven temperature 190°C, 375°F, Gas 5

sesame-
pepper
crackers

Method:
1 Place rice flour or flour, sesame seeds, sage and peppercorns in a bowl and mix to combine.
2 Combine mascarpone and tasty (mature Cheddar) cheese. Add cheese mixture to dry ingredients and mix to form a soft dough.
3 Turn dough onto a lightly floured surface, knead briefly and roll mixture into a sausage shape. Wrap in plastic food wrap and refrigerate for 40 minutes or until firm.
4 Cut into 1cm/¹/₂in-thick slices, place on lightly greased baking trays and brush with egg. Bake for 10 minutes or until biscuits are golden and crisp. Transfer to wire racks to cool.
Note: Mascarpone is made from cream. Unsalted and buttery with a fat content of 90 per cent, it is mostly used as a dessert cheese, either alone or as an ingredient. If it is unavailable, mix one part thick sour cream with three parts lightly whipped thickened (double) cream , or beat 250g/8oz ricotta cheese with 250mL/8fl oz pure (single) cream until the mixture is smooth and thick.
Makes 30

ingredients

1 cup/185g/6oz rice flour or
1 cup/125g/4oz flour, sifted
2 tablespoons sesame seeds, toasted
1 tablespoon chopped fresh sage or
1 teaspoon dried sage
2 teaspoons pink peppercorns, crushed
125g/4oz mascarpone
60g/2oz grated tasty (mature Cheddar) cheese
1 egg, lightly beaten

mexican
cornbread

Method:

1 *Place cornmeal flour (polenta), all-purpose flour and baking powder in a bowl. Add tasty (mature Cheddar) cheese , Parmesan cheese, olives, sun- dried tomatoes, sweet corn and green capsicums (peppers) in a bowl and mix to combine.*

2 *Combine eggs, milk, yoghurt and oil. Add egg mixture to dry ingredients and mix until just combined.*

3 *Pour mixture into a greased 20cm/8in springform pan and bake for I hour or until bread is cooked when tested with a skewer. Serve warm or cold.*

Note: *Split wedges of this loaf and layer with savoury fillings to create attractive sandwiches. This cornbread is also delicious served warm and topped with baked ricotta cheese.*

Makes one 20cm/8in round loaf

ingredients

2 cups/350g/IIoz cornmeal flour (polenta)
2 cups/250g/8oz all purpose flour, sifted
2¹/₂teaspoons baking powder
125g/4oz grated tasty
(mature Cheddar) cheese
60g/2oz grated Parmesan cheese
12 pitted black olives, sliced
12 sun-dried tomatoes, chopped
100g/3¹/₂oz canned sweet corn
kernels, drained
3 bottled green capsicums (peppers),
chopped finely
2 eggs, lightly beaten
I cup/250ml/8fl oz milk
³/₄ cup/155g/5oz yoghurt
¹/₄ cup/60ml/2fl oz vegetable oil

Oven temperature 180°C, 350°F, Gas 4

ham-mustard
scrolls

Method:

1 *Place flour, baking powder and butter in a food processor and process until mixture resembles coarse breadcrumbs. With machine running, slowly add egg and milk and process to form a soft dough. Turn dough onto a lightly floured surface and press out to make a 1cm/¹/₂in-thick rectangle.*

2 *To make filling, place ham, ricotta cheese, tasty (mature Cheddar) cheese and mustard into a bowl and mix to combine. Spread filling over dough and roll up from short side.*

3 *Using a serrated edged knife, cut roll into 2cm/³/₄in thick slices and place on a lightly greased and floured baking tray. Bake for 15-20 minutes or until puffed and golden.*

Note: *These tangy scone pinwheels make an interesting accompaniment to egg dishes at breakfast or brunch. They can also be reheated briefly in the microwave oven for an afternoon snack.*

Makes 18

ingredients

2 cups/250g/8oz plain flour, sifted
2¹/₂ teaspoon baking powder, sifted
60g/2oz butter, chopped
1 egg, lightly beaten
¹/₂ cup/125ml/4fl oz milk
Ham and mustard filling
4 slices smoked ham, chopped
¹/₂ cup/125g/4oz ricotta cheese, drained
**60g/2oz grated tasty
(mature Cheddar) cheese**
2 tablespoons wholegrain mustard

thumbprint
cookies

Photograph opposite

ingredients

Method:

1 *Place butter, icing sugar and vanilla essence in a bowl and beat until light and fluffy. Sift together flour, baking powder and custard powder. Fold flour mixture and milk, alternately, into butter mixture.*

2 *Roll tablespoons of mixture into balls and place on greased baking trays. Make a thumbprint in the centre of each cookie.*

3 *Fill thumbprint hole with a teaspoon of jam, lemon curd or chocolate. Bake for 12 minutes or until cookies are golden. Transfer to wire racks to cool.*

Note: *Wrap the dough in plastic food wrap and chill at least 30 minutes to make it easier to shape into balls. For a subtle toasty nut flavour, roll the balls in sesame seeds before making the thumbprint and filling.*

Makes 30

185g/6oz butter, softened
1/3 cup/45g/1 1/2oz icing sugar, sifted
1 teaspoon vanilla essence
1 teaspoon baking powder
1 1/2 cup/185g/6oz all purpose flour
1/2 cup/60g/2oz custard powder
1/4 cup/60ml/2fl oz milk
jam, lemon curd or chopped chocolate

Oven temperature 190°C, 375°F, Gas 5

monte carlo
biscuits

Photograph opposite

ingredients

Method:

1 *Place butter, brown sugar and vanilla essence in a bowl and beat until light and fluffy. Add egg, flour, baking powder, coconut and rolled oats and mix well to combine.*

2 *Roll tablespoons of mixture into balls, place on greased baking trays and flatten slightly with a fork. Bake for 12 minutes or until biscuits are golden. Transfer to wire racks to cool.*

3 *To make Butter Cream, place butter, icing sugar and vanilla essence in a bowl and beat until light and fluffy. Spread half the biscuits with raspberry jam and top with Butter cream. Top with remaining biscuits.*

Note: *When shaping the biscuits ensure that all are of uniform size and appearance so that each pair is perfectly matched when sandwiched together.*

Makes 20

125g/4oz butter, softened
1 cup/170g/5 1/2oz brown sugar
2 teaspoons vanilla essence
1 egg, lightly beaten
1 1/2 cup/185g/6oz flour, sifted
1 teaspoon baking powder
90g/3oz desiccated coconut
3/4 cup/75g/2 1/2oz rolled oats
1/2 cup/155g/5oz raspberry jam
<u>Butter cream</u>
60g/2oz butter, softened
1/2 cup/75g/2 1/2oz icing sugar
1 teaspoon vanilla essence

Oven temperature 190°C, 375°F, Gas 5

pecan & cherry
bread

Method:

1 *Beat egg whites until soft peaks form, gradually beat in sugar. Continue beating until mixture is firm and glossy. Fold through the sifted flour, pecans and cherries. Mix well. Spoon mixture into a grease 8cmx18cm/3x7in loaf pan*

2 *Bake in an oven 180°C/350°F for 30 minutes or until golden and firm to touch.*

3 *Cool cake in tin. Wrap in foil and refrigerate overnight. Next day cut the cake into thin slices and place on an ungreased baking tray. Bake in an oven 150°C/300°F until light and golden in colour. Cool. Store in an air tight container.*

4 *Serve with coffee or as a biscuit with ice cream.*

ingredients

3 egg whites
1/2 cup/120g/4oz castor sugar
1 cup/120g/4oz plain flour
3/4 cup/90g/3oz pecan halves
1/2 cup/120g/4oz glacé cherries, cut in half

Oven temperature 180°C, 350°F, Gas 4

gingerbread
people

Method:

1 Cream together the margarine and brown sugar, and beat in the egg yolk, mixing well. Sift in the flour, bicarbonate of soda and ginger and gradually blend into the creamed mixture, along with the golden syrup. Knead lightly to make a soft dough.

2 Divide the dough into small portions. Roll out each portion of dough to a thickness of ¹/₂ cm/¹/₄in between two sheets of greaseproof paper. Cut into shapes using cutters.

3 Place on lightly greased oven trays. Bake in a 180°C/350°F oven for 10 minutes. Cool on trays.

Makes approximately 20 shapes (depending on size)

ingredients

125g/4oz margarine
¹/₂ cup/75g/2¹/₂oz brown sugar
1 egg yolk
2¹/₂ cups/300g/10oz plain flour
1 teaspoon bicarbonate of soda
3 teaspoons ginger ground
2¹/₂ tablespoons golden syrup

fig pinwheel
biscuits

Oven temperature 180°C, 350°F, Gas 4

1

2

3

ingredients

170g/5¹/₂oz butter
1 cup/170g/5¹/₂oz brown sugar
1 egg
¹/₂ teaspoon vanilla essence
3 cups/375g/12oz flour
¹/₂ teaspoon bicarbonate of soda
¹/₄ teaspoon ground cinnamon
¹/₄ teaspoon ground nutmeg
2 tablespoons milk
Fig and almond filling
**250g/8oz dried figs,
finely chopped**
¹/₄ cup/60g/2oz sugar
**¹/₂ cup/125mL/4fl oz
water**
**¹/₄ teaspoon ground
mixed spice**
**30g/1oz almonds,
finely chopped**

Method:

1 *To make filling, place figs, sugar, water and mixed spice in a saucepan and bring to the boil. Reduce heat and cook, stirring, for 2-3 minutes or until mixture is thick. Remove pan from heat and stir in almonds. Set aside to cool.*

2 *Place butter in a bowl and beat until light and fluffy. Gradually add sugar, beating well after each addition until mixture is creamy. Beat in egg and vanilla essence.*

3 *Sift together flour, bicarbonate of soda, cinnamon and nutmeg. Beat milk and half the flour mixture into butter mixture. Stir in remaining flour mixture. Turn dough onto a lightly floured surface and knead briefly. Roll into a ball, wrap in plastic food wrap and refrigerate for 30 minutes.*

4 *Divide dough into two portions. Roll one portion out to a 20x28cm/8x11in rectangle and spread with half the filling. Roll up like a*

Swiss roll from the long side. Repeat with remaining dough and filling. Wrap rolls in plastic food wrap and refrigerate for 15 minutes or until you are ready to cook the biscuits.

5 *Cut rolls into 1cm/¹/₂in-thick slices. Place slices on lightly greased baking trays and bake for 10-12 minutes. Stand biscuits on trays for 1 minute before removing to wire racks to cool completely.*

Note: *The uncooked rolls can be frozen if you wish. When you have unexpected guests, or the biscuit barrel is empty, these biscuits are great standbys.*

Makes 50

palmiers

1

2

3

ingredients

170g/5¹/₂oz prepared puff pastry
15g/¹/₂oz butter, melted and cooled
3 tablespoons demerara sugar

Method:

1 Roll out pastry to make a 25cm/10in square, 3cm/1¹/₈in thick.
2 Brush with butter and sprinkle with a little sugar. Fold two opposite edges of pastry half way towards the centre.
3 Sprinkle with a little more sugar and fold, taking edges to the centre. Sprinkle with a more sugar and fold one half of pastry over the other half. Press lightly to join.
4 Cut pastry roll into 18 slices and place on a greased baking tray. Flatten slightly and bake for 10-15 minutes or until puffed and golden.

Pistachio Palmiers:
Combine 15g/¹/₂oz finely chopped unsalted pistachio nuts and 3 tablespoons soft brown sugar, and sprinkle over pastry in place of the demerara sugar.

Almond Palmiers:
Combine 3 tablespoons ground almonds, 2 tablespoons caster sugar and 1 teaspoon ground mixed spice and sprinkle over pastry in place of the demerara sugar.

Note: The secret to making these heart-shaped pastries is in the way that the pastry is folded. Palmiers are a great way to use left over puff pastry. Try sandwiching the palmierstogether with whipped cream. Delicious!

Makes 18

Cooking is not an exact science: one does not require finely calibrated scales, pipettes and scientific equipment to cook, yet the conversion to metric measures in some countries and its interpretations must have intimidated many a good cook.

Weights are given in the recipes only for ingredients such as meats, fish, poultry and some vegetables. Though a few grams/ounces one way or another will not affect the success of your dish.

Though recipes have been tested using the Australian Standard 250mL cup, 20mL tablespoon and 5mL teaspoon, they will work just as well with the US and Canadian 8fl oz cup, or the UK 300mL cup. We have used graduated cup measures in preference to tablespoon measures so that proportions are always the same. Where tablespoon measures have been given, these are not crucial measures, so using the smaller tablespoon of the US or UK will not affect the recipe's success. At least we all agree on the teaspoon size.

For breads, cakes, pastries, etc the only area which might cause concern is where eggs are used, as proportions will then vary. If working with a 250mL or 300mL cup, use large eggs (60g/2oz), adding a little more liquid to the recipe for 300mL cup measures if it seems necessary. Use the medium-sized eggs (55g/1 $^{1}/_{4}$oz) with 8fl oz cup measure. A graduated set of measuring cups and spoons is recommended, the cups in particular for measuring dry ingredients. Remember to level such ingredients.

English measures

All measurements are similar to Australian with two exceptions: the English cup measures 300mL/10fl-oz, whereas the Australian cup measure 250mL/8fl ozs. The English tablespoon (the Australian dessertspoon) measures 14.8mL against the Australian tablespoon of 20mL.

American measures

The American reputed pint is 16fl oz, a quart is equal to 32fl oz and the American gallon, 128fl oz. The Imperial measurement is 20fl oz to the pint, 40 fl oz a quart and 160 floz one gallon.

The American tablespoon is equal to 14.8mL, the teaspoon is 5mL. The cup measure is 250mL/8 fl oz, the same as Australia.

Dry measures

All the measures are level, so when you have filled a cup or spoon, level it off with the edge of a knife. The scale below is the "cook's equivalent", it is not an exact conversion of metric to imperial measurement.

The exact metric equivalent is 2.2046lb = 1kg or 1lb = 0.45359kg

Metric		Imperial	
g = grams		oz = ounces	
kg = kilograms		lb = pound	
15g		$^{1}/_{2}$oz	
20g		$^{2}/_{3}$oz	
30g		1oz	
60g		2oz	
90g		3oz	
125g		4oz	$^{1}/_{4}$lb
155g		5oz	
185g		6oz	
220g		7oz	
250g		8oz	$^{1}/_{2}$lb
280g		9oz	
315g		10oz	
345g		11oz	
375g		12oz	$^{3}/_{4}$lb
410g		13oz	
440g		14oz	
470g		15oz	
1000g	1kg	35.2oz	2.2lb
	1.5kg		3.3lb

Oven temperatures

The Celsius temperatures given here are not exact; they have been rounded off and are given as a guide only. Follow the manufacturer's temperature guide, relating it to oven description given in the recipe. Remember gas ovens are hottest at the top, electric ovens at the bottom and convection-fan forced ovens are usually even throughout. We included Regulo numbers for gas cookers which may assist. To convert °C to °F multiply °C by 9 and divide by 5 then add 32.

Oven temperatures

	C°	F°	Regulo
Very slow	120	250	1
Slow	150	300	2
Moderately slow	150	325	3
Moderate	180	350	4
Moderately hot	190-200	370-400	5-6
Hot	210-220	410-440	6-7
Very hot	230	450	8
Super hot	250-290	475-500	9-10

Cake dish sizes

Metric	Imperial
15cm	6in
18cm	7in
20cm	8in
23cm	9in

Loaf dish sizes

Metric	Imperial
23x12cm	9x5in
25x8cm	10x3in
28x18cm	11x7in

Liquid measures

Metric	Imperial	Cup & Spoon
mL	fl oz	
millilitres	fluid ounce	
5mL	$^1/_6$fl oz	1 teaspoon
20mL	$^2/_3$fl oz	1 tablespoon
30mL	1fl oz	1 tablespoon plus 2 teaspoons
60mL	2fl oz	$^1/_4$ cup
85mL	2$^1/_2$fl oz	$^1/_3$ cup
100mL	3fl oz	$^3/_8$ cup
125mL	4fl oz	$^1/_2$ cup
150mL	5fl oz	$^1/_4$ pint, 1 gill
250mL	8fl oz	1 cup
300mL	10fl oz	$^1/_2$ pint)
360mL	12fl oz	1$^1/_2$ cups
420mL	14fl oz	1$^3/_4$ cups
500mL	16fl oz	2 cups
600mL	20fl oz 1 pint,	2$^1/_2$ cups
1 litre	35fl oz 1 $^3/_4$ pints,	4 cups

Cup measurements

One cup is equal to the following weights.

	Metric	Imperial
Almonds, flaked	90g	3oz
Almonds, slivered, ground	125g	4oz
Almonds, kernel	155g	5oz
Apples, dried, chopped	125g	4oz
Apricots, dried, chopped	190g	6oz
Breadcrumbs, packet	125g	4oz
Breadcrumbs, soft	60g	2oz
Cheese, grated	125g	4oz
Choc bits	155g	5oz
Coconut, desiccated	90g	3oz
Cornflakes	30g	1oz
Currants	155g	5oz
Flour	125g	4oz
Fruit, dried (mixed, sultanas etc)	185g	6oz
Ginger, crystallised, glace	250g	8oz
Honey, treacle, golden syrup	315g	10oz
Mixed peel	220g	7oz
Nuts, chopped	125g	4oz
Prunes, chopped	220g	7oz
Rice, cooked	155g	5oz
Rice, uncooked	220g	7oz
Rolled oats	90g	3oz
Sesame seeds	125g	4oz
Shortening (butter, margarine)	250g	8oz
Sugar, brown	155g	5oz
Sugar, granulated or caster	250g	8oz
Sugar, sifted icing	155g	5oz
Wheatgerm	60g	2oz

Length

Some of us are still having trouble converting imperial to metric. In this scale measures have been rounded off to the easiest-to-use and most acceptable figures.

To obtain the exact metric equivalent to convert inches to centimetres, multiply inches by 2.54 Therefore 1 inch equal 25.4 millimetres and 1 millimetre equal 0.03937 inches.

Metric	Imperial
mm=millimetres	in = inches
cm=centimetres	ft = feet
5mm, 0.5cm	$^1/_4$in
10mm, 1.0cm	$^1/_2$in
20mm, 2.0cm	$^3/_4$in
2.5cm	1in
5cm	2in
8cm	3in
10cm	4in
12cm	5in
15cm	6in
18cm	7in
20cm	8in
23cm	9in
25cm	10in
28cm	11in
30cm	1 ft, 12in